I0076921

RICH KID
POOR KID
THE FIRST $1000

ANTHONY CARMICHAEL

Copyright © 2025 by Anthony Carmichael.

All rights reserved. No part of this publication may be reproduced, distributed, or transmitted in any form or by any means, including photocopying, recording, or other electronic or mechanical methods, without the prior written permission of the publisher, except in the case of brief quotations embodied in critical reviews and certain other non-commercial uses permitted by copyright law. For permission requests, write to the publisher, addressed "Attention: Permissions Coordinator," at the address below.

Million Minds Investment Group

[8-9251 Yonge St. Suite # 412---Richmond Hill, ONTARIO L4C-9T3]

https://www.richkidpoorkidbooks.com

ISBN: [978-1-7389976-4-0]

Printed in Canada

Disclaimer: The information contained in this book is for educational and informational purposes only. It is not intended to be a substitute for professional financial advice. The author and publisher disclaim any liability for any decisions you may make based on the information contained herein. You should consult a financial advisor before making any financial decisions.

📕 The First $1,000 – Structure

🏗 Part 1: Mindset & Foundation

💼 Part 2: Making Your First $1,000

📚 Bonus Sections

Dedication

To every dreamer who's ever looked at their bank account and thought, *"There's got to be more than this."*

This book is for you. The first $1,000 isn't just money — it's proof that you can create your own path, build your own wealth, and rewrite your own story.

Preface:
Why This Book Matters

When I wrote *Rich Kid, Poor Kid*, it wasn't just a book about money — it was about mindset. About showing that financial freedom isn't reserved for the lucky few, but for anyone willing to learn the habits and put in the work.

This book continues that mission but zooms in on one of the most powerful milestones you'll ever hit: your first $1,000.

Why $1,000? Because it's the turning point. It's the proof that you don't have to wait for a raise, a lottery ticket, or a miracle. You can create money, opportunities, and momentum from scratch. And once you've done it once, you'll never look at money the same way again.

This is more than a guide — it's a blueprint. Follow it, take action, and watch your first $1,000 become the foundation of the life you've always wanted.

Introduction:
Why the First $1,000 Changes Everything

The first $1,000 is special. It's not just cash — it's confidence. It's proof that your ideas, skills, and hustle can turn into real money.

For some, that $1,000 pays off debt. For others, it's the start of an emergency fund. For many, it's the seed that grows into a business. But no matter how you use it, the first $1,000 will flip a switch in your mind: *If I can do this once, I can do it again. And again. And again.*

That's how everyday millionaires are made. Not by winning the lottery, but by stacking small wins into big ones.

This book will show you the path. Hustles you can start today. Habits you can build right now. Systems that take you from broke and stuck to confident and in control.

How to Use This Book

This isn't a book you just read — it's a book you **do.**

Here's how to get the most out of it:

1. **Pick one hustle at a time.** Don't try to do everything at once. Focus, test, learn, and grow.

2. **Track your progress.** Write down what works, what doesn't, and how much you earn.

3. **Stack wins.** $100 becomes $500. $500 becomes $1,000. Each small victory builds momentum.

4. **Build habits, not just hustles.** This book isn't about quick cash only — it's about creating the mindset and systems that will carry you far beyond $1,000.

5. **Take action immediately.** Don't just highlight ideas — apply them today. Even if it's one small step, momentum matters more than perfection.

Follow the steps, trust the process, and you'll soon realize: the first $1,000 isn't the end — it's the beginning of your financial freedom story.

🏗️ Part 1:

Mindset & Foundation

💡 Chapter 1:
The First Step – Why $1,000 Is a Game-Changer

If you're holding this book, chances are you've felt that squeeze before. Bills pile up. Prices keep rising. Your paycheck feels like it's already spent the moment it lands. The idea of building wealth might even feel impossible when you're stuck at zero.

But here's the truth: the first $1,000 changes everything.

🔑 Why $1,000 Matters So Much

- **It's Proof of Concept.** Once you make that first $1,000 outside your job, you prove to yourself that money can come from you — your skills, your creativity, your hustle — not just an employer.

- **It Builds Confidence.** That first stack makes you say, *"If I did this once, I can do it again."* Confidence turns into momentum. Momentum turns into wealth.

- **It Creates Options.** With $1,000, you can pay down debt, start investing, buy tools, or launch the next hustle. Options equal freedom.
- **It Breaks Limiting Beliefs.** Poor Kid thinking says, *"I can't."* Rich Kid thinking says, *"I just did."*

⚡ The Psychological Shift

Most people underestimate the mental shift that happens after their first $1,000. It's not about the number — it's about what it represents.

- Suddenly, money feels possible.
- Suddenly, you're in control, not just reacting to bills.
- Suddenly, you realize wealth isn't for "other people" — it's for you too.

That's the **game-changer.** You stop waiting for permission and start writing your own financial story.

☑️ Why $1,000 Beats a Raise

Think about this: if your boss gave you a raise of $1,000 per year, that's less than $20/week after taxes. But when you

create $1,000 on your own terms, you open the door to repeat it as many times as you want.

- A raise is capped.
- A hustle is unlimited.

Everyday millionaires know this. That's why they build streams of income — because one stream can dry up, but many streams flow forever.

🚀 What This Book Will Do

This isn't a book of theory. It's a playbook. I'm going to give you:

- Practical hustles you can start right away.
- Step-by-step money moves to grow your stack.
- Habits that turn $1,000 into $10,000, and $10,000 into $100,000.

The journey to becoming an everyday millionaire starts with your first $1,000. And once you hit it, you'll never see money the same way again.

💡 Everyday Millionaire Mindset

Don't downplay your first $1,000. Don't shrug it off like "just a little extra." Treat it like your first brick in the empire you're building. Because when you stack bricks long enough, you don't just have money — you have a fortress of freedom.

🧠 Chapter 2:
Rich Kid vs. Poor Kid Thinking — Habits That Win Early

Money isn't just numbers in a bank account — it's habits in your daily life. Before you ever see your first $1,000 stack up, the habits you practice will either set you up for success or quietly sabotage you.

This is where the difference between a "Rich Kid" and a "Poor Kid" becomes clear. It's not about who was born with more. It's about how they **think, act, and use money** on a daily basis.

⚖️ Rich Kid vs. Poor Kid Thinking

- **Poor Kid Thinking:** "I'll start when I have more money."
- **Rich Kid Thinking:** "I'll start with what I have and make it grow."
- **Poor Kid Thinking:** Spends money as fast as it comes in.

- **Rich Kid Thinking:** Tells money where to go before it even arrives.
- **Poor Kid Thinking:** Sees money as survival.
- **Rich Kid Thinking:** Sees money as a tool for freedom.

⚒ The Habits That Win Early

1. **Track Every Dollar**

   Poor Kid ignores where the money goes. Rich Kid watches it like a coach studies game film. Use a notebook, an app, or even sticky notes. The goal is awareness.

2. **Pay Yourself First**

   Even if it's just $10, Rich Kid habits mean setting aside money before you spend it. That $10 grows into $100, then $1,000, then freedom.

3. **Invest in Skills, Not Just Stuff**

   Poor Kid buys the latest gadget. Rich Kid buys a course, a book, or a tool that creates income. Skills pay forever.

4. **Delay Gratification**

   Rich Kid doesn't need the instant reward. They'll wait,

stack, and multiply before spending. Poor Kid says, *"I deserve it now."* Rich Kid says, *"I'll deserve it when my money earns it for me."*

5. **Stay Curious, Stay Learning**

   Poor Kid assumes they know enough. Rich Kid stays a student of money, hustles, and opportunities. They learn, apply, adjust, and win.

🔑 Why Habits Beat Hustle Alone

Hustle makes money. Habits keep money. Without habits, even the best hustle collapses. How many athletes, entertainers, or lottery winners went broke? Hustle gave them the money, but poor habits drained it.

💡 **Millionaire Reminder:** A strong hustle with weak habits equals failure. A small hustle with strong habits equals growth.

🦴 Everyday Millionaire Mindset

Think of habits like seeds. They don't look like much at first, but over time, they grow into something massive. The early habits you plant today will determine the financial forest you walk through tomorrow.

So, ask yourself: are you planting weeds or are you planting wealth?

📊 Chapter 3:
The $1,000 Blueprint – Breaking Down the Goal

$1,000 might sound big when you're starting from zero. But when you break it down, it becomes clear: $1,000 isn't some far-off dream — it's just a series of smaller wins stacked together.

Here's the blueprint.

🍀 Step 1: Break $1,000 Into Bite-Sized Pieces

- $1,000 = 10 projects at $100 each
- $1,000 = 20 gigs at $50 each
- $1,000 = 100 quick wins at $10 each

It's not about making $1,000 in one shot — it's about stacking small wins until they add up.

💡 **Millionaire Mindset:** Every $10 counts. Don't disrespect small amounts — they build big stacks.

⏱ Step 2: Break It Down by Time

- **$33 a day** for 30 days = $1,000

- **$125 a week** for 8 weeks = $1,000

- **$250 every weekend** for a month = $1,000

Suddenly the goal isn't "make $1,000." It's: *How can I make $33 today?*

🎯 Step 3: Match Hustles to Your Numbers

- Need $33/day? → Pet sitting, tutoring, delivery apps.

- Need $125/week? → Weekend photography, furniture flipping, reselling online.

- Need $500 in 2 weeks? → Freelancing, lawn care, or local service hustles.

The hustle you pick depends on how fast you want to hit the milestone.

💼 Step 4: Use the 3 Hustle Categories

Think of hustles like tools:

1. **Quick Cash Hustles** – Small, fast, repeatable (delivery apps, babysitting, odd jobs).

2. **Medium Hustles** – Higher skill or effort, medium payouts (freelancing, reselling, tutoring).

3. **Scaling Hustles** – Systems that can be repeated or built bigger (online stores, digital products).

Mix and match them depending on your timeframe.

🔑 Step 5: Stack, Don't Stall

Here's the trap: people get $100, then they blow it. Or they make $500, then stop. But the first $1,000 only happens if you keep stacking. Don't lose momentum halfway.

💡 **Pro Tip:** Keep a visible tracker (whiteboard, notebook, app) where you mark every $10 or $100 earned. Seeing progress keeps the fire lit.

🌑 Everyday Millionaire Blueprint

Wealth is just small wins stacked over time. That $1,000 is your training ground. If you can hit it once, you can hit it twice. If you can hit it twice, you can hit $10,000. And if you can hit $10,000? You're already on the road to six figures. The blueprint is simple: break it down, hustle it up, stack it high.

💼 Part 2:
Making Your First $1,000

⚡ Chapter 4:
Quick Wins – Fast Cash Hustles Anyone Can Do

Not every hustle takes months to build. Some can put money in your pocket **today.** Quick wins aren't always the biggest earners, but they're powerful because they build momentum. They give you proof that your time and skills are valuable.

If your goal is $1,000, quick wins are the stepping stones that get you there faster.

🚗 1. Delivery Driving (Food & Groceries)

Description: Drive for apps like Uber Eats, DoorDash, or Instacart.

Startup Cost: $–$$ (car, bike, or scooter).

Time Commitment: Flexible.

Income Potential: $50–$150/day depending on hours.

Pro Tip: Work lunch, dinner, and weekend peaks — those hours pay the most.

🐶 2. Pet Sitting & Dog Walking

Description: Care for pets while owners are busy or traveling.

Startup Cost: $ (leash, basic supplies).

Time Commitment: Flexible.

Income Potential: $15–$25 per walk; $30–$75 per overnight stay.

Pro Tip: Use apps like Rover and Wag! to get started instantly.

🧹 3. House Cleaning

Description: Offer cleaning services for busy households or small offices.

Startup Cost: $–$$ (supplies).

Time Commitment: Flexible.

Income Potential: $100–$300 per job.

Pro Tip: Offer discounts for weekly or bi-weekly clients to secure repeat income.

🛍️ 4. Reselling Unused Stuff

Description: Sell clothes, electronics, or furniture you don't use.

Startup Cost: $ (inventory already owned).

Time Commitment: Flexible.

Income Potential: $50–$500+ quickly.

Pro Tip: List on multiple platforms (Facebook Marketplace, eBay, Poshmark) for faster sales.

📷 5. Freelance Photography

Description: Offer event, portrait, or product photography.

Startup Cost: $$ (camera gear or even a good smartphone).

Time Commitment: Part-time.

Income Potential: $100–$500/session.

Pro Tip: Start with friends/family to build a portfolio.

⚒ 6. Odd Jobs & Task Apps

Description: Help people move, assemble furniture, or run errands via TaskRabbit or Craigslist.

Startup Cost: $ (basic tools).

Time Commitment: Flexible.

Income Potential: $20–$100/hour depending on the task.

Pro Tip: Specialize in quick jobs like IKEA assembly — huge demand.

📟 7. Tutoring (Online or In-Person)

Description: Help students with math, science, or language skills.

Startup Cost: $ (knowledge + internet).

Time Commitment: Flexible.

Income Potential: $20–$100/hour.

Pro Tip: Focus on test prep — parents pay more for results.

🎤 8. Gig Work (Fiverr/Upwork)

Description: Offer skills like writing, design, or voiceover.

Startup Cost: $ (just your laptop).

Time Commitment: Flexible.

Income Potential: $10–$200 per gig.

Pro Tip: Start small and build reviews, then raise your rates.

🎊 9. Babysitting / Childcare

Description: Watch kids for neighbors, friends, or local families.

Startup Cost: $ (basic toys, CPR certification boosts credibility).

Time Commitment: Flexible/part-time.

Income Potential: $15–$30/hour; more for overnights.

Pro Tip: Market yourself as "last-minute reliable" — parents love it.

🛒 10. Flipping Thrift Finds

Description: Buy undervalued items from thrift stores or garage sales, then resell them.

Startup Cost: $–$$ (inventory).

Time Commitment: Flexible.

Income Potential: $100–$1,000+/month.

Pro Tip: Look for high-demand categories like vintage clothing or sneakers.

⬤ Everyday Millionaire Mindset

Quick wins aren't about getting rich overnight — they're about proving to yourself that you **can** create money. Once you've felt that first hustle paycheck hit your hand, you'll never see yourself the same way again.

Your goal isn't to stop at quick wins — it's to use them as fuel. $50 today. $200 this week. Before you know it, you're staring at your first $1,000.

💵 Chapter 5:
The $100 Hustle – Small Gigs That Add Up Big

Making $20 here and $40 there is cool — but when you start landing **$100 gigs**, that's when the first $1,000 feels within reach. Small but solid hustles stack up quickly, and they build the skills and reputation that push you into bigger opportunities.

🎨 1. Graphic Design Gigs

Description: Design logos, flyers, or social media posts for local businesses.

Startup Cost: $ (Canva or free design tools).

Time Commitment: Part-time.

Income Potential: $100–$500/project.

Pro Tip: Offer packages (logo + social media graphics) to hit $100+ easily.

🔧 2. Furniture Assembly / Handyman Tasks

Description: Help people assemble IKEA furniture or handle small repairs.

Startup Cost: $–$$ (basic tools).

Time Commitment: Flexible.

Income Potential: $50–$150 per gig.

Pro Tip: List services on TaskRabbit and Facebook Marketplace.

📷 3. Mini Photo Sessions

Description: Offer 30-minute portrait sessions for families, graduates, or couples.

Startup Cost: $$ (camera or smartphone with tripod).

Time Commitment: 1–2 hours per gig.

Income Potential: $100–$300 per session.

Pro Tip: Do seasonal promos — "holiday photos," "back-to-school portraits," etc.

🐕 4. Weekend Pet Care

Description: Watch pets while owners are away for the weekend.

Startup Cost: $ (supplies like treats, toys).

Time Commitment: Flexible.

Income Potential: $100–$250 per weekend.

Pro Tip: Offer daily photo updates to earn trust and repeat bookings.

5. Private Tutoring

Description: Teach math, science, or language one-on-one.

Startup Cost: $ (internet + knowledge).

Time Commitment: Flexible.

Income Potential: $30–$75/hour (so 2–4 hours = $100).

Pro Tip: Specialize in high-demand subjects like SAT/ACT prep or college admissions.

6. Event Hosting / DJ Gigs

Description: Provide music or hosting for small parties or community events.

Startup Cost: $$ (basic sound system or rentals).

Time Commitment: A few hours per event.

Income Potential: $100–$500/event.

Pro Tip: Offer MC + playlist management for budget clients who can't afford big DJs.

🖊 7. Freelance Writing

Description: Write blog posts, website copy, or product descriptions.

Startup Cost: $ (laptop).

Time Commitment: Flexible.

Income Potential: $50–$200/article.

Pro Tip: Specialize in one niche (fitness, finance, tech) to stand out and charge more.

🚚 8. Moving Help

Description: Help people pack, lift, or transport belongings.

Startup Cost: $–$$ (dolly, straps).

Time Commitment: Half-day or weekend.

Income Potential: $100–$300 per move.

Pro Tip: Market as "last-minute moving help" — people pay a premium when stressed.

🍪 9. Baked Goods or Catering Small Orders

Description: Sell baked goods for birthdays, office parties, or community events.

Startup Cost: $$ (ingredients, packaging).

Time Commitment: Part-time.

Income Potential: $50–$200/order.

Pro Tip: Focus on custom orders (cupcakes, themed cakes) where people will pay extra.

💻 10. Tech Help & Setup

Description: Help people set up laptops, smartphones, or smart home devices.

Startup Cost: $ (your know-how).

Time Commitment: Flexible.

Income Potential: $50–$150/gig.

Pro Tip: Market to seniors or small businesses who need patient, clear help.

⚫ Everyday Millionaire Mindset

The $100 hustle is about consistency. One gig won't make you rich, but 10 gigs will hit your first $1,000. More importantly, these gigs prove that your **skills and time have serious value.**

The difference between a poor kid and a rich kid isn't talent — it's recognizing that even small opportunities can stack into big results when you stay consistent.

💼 Chapter 6:
The $500 Hustle – Medium Plays That Scale Fast

By now, you've seen how quick wins and $100 gigs stack into momentum. But what if you want to hit your first $1,000 even faster? That's where the **$500 hustle** comes in.

These aren't one-off gigs. They're bigger projects, small businesses, or systems that can pay you in chunks of hundreds — sometimes in a single weekend. They take more planning, but the reward is worth it.

📷 1. Event Photography or Videography

Description: Shoot weddings, birthdays, or corporate events.

Startup Cost: $$–$$$ (camera gear or rentals).

Time Commitment: A full day + editing.

Income Potential: $500–$2,000 per event.

Pro Tip: Start with small events (birthday parties) to build your portfolio, then move into weddings.

🚚 2. Moving Service (Small-Scale)

Description: Offer a "two men and a truck" type service locally.

Startup Cost: $$–$$$ (truck rental + equipment).

Time Commitment: A few hours to a full day.

Income Potential: $300–$1,000 per move.

Pro Tip: Target college move-in/move-out seasons or post-lease months for high demand.

🍽 3. Catering or Meal Prep Service

Description: Cook and deliver meals for small parties, events, or busy families.

Startup Cost: $$ (ingredients, permits, packaging).

Time Commitment: Part-time/full-time.

Income Potential: $200–$1,000+ per order.

Pro Tip: Specialize in dietary niches (keto, vegan, gluten-free) for premium pricing.

🪑 4. Furniture Flipping (Bigger Items)

Description: Refinish, repaint, or repurpose large furniture pieces and resell.

Startup Cost: $$ (used furniture + tools).

Time Commitment: Flexible.

Income Potential: $200–$1,000 per flip.

Pro Tip: Target trendy styles (farmhouse, mid-century modern) for faster sales.

🏠 5. Airbnb / Short-Term Rental

Description: Rent out a spare room, basement, or property.

Startup Cost: $$–$$$ (cleaning, furnishing).

Time Commitment: Low (after setup).

Income Potential: $500–$3,000/month depending on location.

Pro Tip: Offer unique experiences (cozy workspace, pet-friendly stays) to stand out.

🎤 6. DJ or Entertainment Services

Description: Provide music and entertainment for parties or local events.

Startup Cost: $$–$$$ (sound system, laptop).

Time Commitment: A few hours.

Income Potential: $500–$2,000 per event.

Pro Tip: Market through wedding planners or event coordinators.

7. Freelance Web Design

Description: Build websites for small businesses.

Startup Cost: $–$$ (laptop, software).

Time Commitment: Part-time/full-time.

Income Potential: $500–$5,000 per project.

Pro Tip: Focus on local small businesses who need simple but professional websites.

8. Art Commissions / Large Projects

Description: Create murals, paintings, or large custom art pieces.

Startup Cost: $$ (materials).

Time Commitment: Flexible.

Income Potential: $300–$2,000 per piece.

Pro Tip: Partner with cafés, gyms, or offices that want wall art.

9. Wholesale Reselling

Description: Buy products in bulk and resell them individually.

Startup Cost: $$–$$$ (inventory).

Time Commitment: Part-time.

Income Potential: $500–$5,000+/month.

Pro Tip: Target niche items (snacks, accessories,

supplements).

10. Specialty Services (Repairs & Upgrades)

Description: Offer focused services like phone repairs, car

detailing, or home upgrades.

Startup Cost: $$ (tools, training).

Time Commitment: Flexible.

Income Potential: $100–$500+ per client.

Pro Tip: Specialize in one service and dominate locally (e.g.,

"fast phone fix in 30 minutes").

Everyday Millionaire Mindset

$500 hustles are about **leverage.** You're not trading hours for

scraps — you're trading skills, resources, or systems for

bigger paydays. They require more effort up front, but they

also teach you the most valuable lesson: your time is worth more than you think.

When you start landing $500 hustles, $1,000 isn't just a dream — it's a weekend away.

◇ Chapter 7:
The $1,000 Hustle – Building a Repeatable System

Making $1,000 once is exciting. Making $1,000 **over and over again** is where your hustle stops being extra cash and starts becoming a machine. The difference? Systems.

A $1,000 hustle isn't about luck, chance, or one-time gigs. It's about creating a repeatable process that you can rely on to generate income whenever you need it.

🛠 Step 1: Pick a Scalable Hustle

Not every hustle has the power to repeat at $1,000+ levels. Choose one that can:

- Be done multiple times (freelance, services).
- Scale with systems (e-commerce, courses).
- Grow with demand (consulting, rentals).

Examples:

- Launching an **online store** that earns $1,000+ monthly.

- Landing a **freelance retainer client** for $1,000/month.
- Running a **local service business** (cleaning, detailing, catering).
- Building a **subscription product** (coaching, digital templates, meal plans).

📊 Step 2: Break Down the Numbers

A $1,000 system is just math.

- Sell 50 items at $20 each = $1,000
- Sell 20 services at $50 each = $1,000
- Land 4 clients at $250 each = $1,000
- Land 1 contract at $1,000 = $1,000

The formula doesn't change. Once you find your winning combo, you repeat it until it becomes automatic.

🔄 Step 3: Build the System

Systems remove guesswork.

- **Attract customers** (ads, social media, word-of-mouth).
- **Deliver consistently** (templates, SOPs, packages).
- **Get paid smoothly** (invoices, PayPal, online checkout).

💡 **Pro Tip:** If you can explain your hustle in a 3-step process, you can turn it into a repeatable business.

👥 Step 4: Automate & Outsource

Your first $1,000 might be all hustle. But if you want it repeatable:

- Automate marketing with social media schedulers or ads.
- Outsource tasks (design, editing, delivery).
- Use digital tools (payment apps, CRM, email lists).

This lets you focus on scaling instead of chasing every sale.

🚀 Step 5: Rinse & Repeat

The beauty of a $1,000 system is that once it works, you don't need to reinvent the wheel.

- Copy the process.
- Improve small details.
- Scale bigger once demand grows.

The hustle becomes a business. The system becomes income security.

💡 Everyday Millionaire Mindset

The first $1,000 is about **proof.** The repeatable $1,000 is about **power.** Once you know how to build and repeat income systems, you'll never fear being broke again. Because you'll know:

"I can create $1,000 on demand."

That's when you stop being just a hustler and start becoming a builder.

💡 Part 3:

Managing the Money

💰 Chapter 8:
Don't Spend It, Stack It — The Power of Saving Your First $1,000

Anyone can make money once. The real winners are the ones who keep it.

Your first $1,000 is more than just cash — it's **proof** that you can hustle, manage, and grow wealth. But here's the trap: most people blow it. New shoes, new phone, fancy dinners — gone in a weekend.

If you want to separate yourself from the average, you have to **stack it, not spend it.**

🧱 Why Saving Your First $1,000 Matters

- It's your **launchpad** — money that can be reinvested into bigger hustles.
- It's your **safety net** — covering emergencies so you don't fall backward.
- It's your **identity shift** — once you see $1,000 sitting, untouched, you'll never want to be broke again.

💡 **Everyday Millionaire Mindset:** Your first $1,000 isn't for spending. It's for building.

🔑 Step 1: Separate the Money

Don't mix your hustle money with your spending money.

- Open a separate savings account.
- Label it "Wealth Account" or "Millionaire Fund."
- Every dollar goes there until you hit $1,000.

This isn't regular savings — this is your **wealth foundation.**

🔑 Step 2: Automate the Habit

- Every time you get paid → skim 10–30% straight to your savings.
- Treat it like a bill. "Pay yourself first" is how rich kids think.
- Even $5 adds up when you stay consistent.

🔑 Step 3: Protect It Like Gold

Don't let your first $1,000 vanish.

- **Emergencies only** (car repair, medical).
- No impulse buys, no "I deserve it."

- If it's not a need or an investment, leave it.

🔑 Step 4: Reinvest Smartly

Once stacked, don't just let it sit forever. Your $1,000 can:

- Buy tools that grow your hustle.

- Pay for ads to expand your reach.

- Fund a small business launch.

- Start your first investment account.

The key: use it to make **more money.**

🧩 Example: The Cycle of Stacking

1. Hustle until you hit $1,000.

2. Save it (don't touch).

3. Reinvest into a better hustle.

4. Repeat the cycle.

Before long, you're not just making $1,000. You're multiplying it.

Everyday Millionaire Mindset

The poor kid sees $1,000 and spends it to "feel rich."

The rich kid sees $1,000 and knows it's just the **first brick** in the empire.

Remember: money is a tool. If you respect the first $1,000, the next $10,000 will respect you.

📈 Chapter 9:
Multiply the Money – Smart Investments for Beginners

Congratulations — you stacked your first $1,000. Now the real magic begins: making money **work for you.**

Poor Kid Thinking: "Money is for spending."

Rich Kid Thinking: "Money is a soldier — I send it out to bring back more."

Investing isn't just for Wall Street suits. Everyday millionaires start small, learn the game, and build their wealth brick by brick.

🛠️ Step 1: Understand the Goal

Investing isn't about getting rich overnight. It's about:

- **Growth** – your money earns money.
- **Protection** – inflation doesn't eat your savings.
- **Freedom** – building income streams beyond your hustle.

💡 Step 2: Beginner-Friendly Ways to Invest Your First $1,000

1. **High-Yield Savings Account (HYSA)**

   - Safe place to park your money with higher interest than a regular bank.

   - Not huge returns, but risk-free and liquid.

   - Great as your "emergency buffer."

2. **Index Funds / ETFs**

   - Basket of stocks (S&P 500, Total Market).

   - Low-cost, low-risk compared to picking individual stocks.

   - Long-term growth: historically 7–10% per year.

   - Apps like Vanguard, Fidelity, or Robinhood make it simple.

3. **Fractional Shares**

   - Don't need thousands to buy into big companies (Amazon, Apple).

   - Buy $10 or $100 slices and grow over time.

4. **Robo-Advisors**

   - Automated apps like Betterment or Wealthsimple manage your investments.

   - Great for beginners who don't want to pick and choose.

5. **Self-Investment (Skills & Tools)**

   - Courses, certifications, software, or gear that helps you **earn more.**

   - ROI can be bigger than stocks — a $200 course could unlock a $20,000 career.

🔑 Step 3: The Power of Compounding

Here's the millionaire's secret:

- $1,000 invested at 10% annual growth = $2,594 in 10 years.
- Add $100/month = $20,000+ in 10 years.
- Small consistent moves = big future stacks.

💡 **Everyday Millionaire Mindset:** Don't just add money — keep it invested and let time do the heavy lifting.

⚠ Step 4: Avoid Rookie Mistakes

- Don't "YOLO" into trendy stocks or crypto without research.
- Don't invest money you can't afford to lose (rent money ≠ investment money).
- Don't chase "get rich quick" promises.

Investing should feel boring, steady, and powerful.

🌐 Everyday Millionaire Mindset

Your first $1,000 isn't the finish line — it's the seed. Rich kids understand that seeds only grow when planted. Poor kids leave their seeds sitting in a jar, or worse, eat them.

Plant your $1,000 wisely, and you'll build habits that make future thousands grow automatically.

🛡️ Chapter 10:
Protect the Bag – Avoiding Mistakes That Drain Your Cash

Offense wins games, but defense wins championships. The same is true with money. Hustling and investing stack your wealth — but one dumb mistake can drain it overnight. Protecting your bag means building habits that keep your money safe, secure, and growing.

⚠️ The Money Drainers You Must Avoid

1. **Lifestyle Creep**
   - The moment you make more money, you start spending more.
   - Instead of stacking, you "upgrade" — bigger phone plan, fancier car, pricier meals.
   - **Rule:** Keep your lifestyle steady until your money multiplies, not just grows.

2. **Impulse Spending**

   - Amazon, fast food, late-night splurges — death by a thousand cuts.
   - $20 here, $50 there = your first $1,000 gone before it compounds.
   - **Hack:** Wait 24 hours before buying anything non-essential.

3. **Bad Debt**

   - Credit cards, payday loans, buy-now-pay-later traps.
   - Interest turns $1,000 into a $3,000 hole.
   - **Rich Kid Move:** Use debt only if it makes you money (like business credit for hustles).

4. **No Emergency Fund**

   - Car breaks down → you dip into investments.
   - Hospital bill → you swipe credit.
   - **Fix:** Keep at least $500–$1,000 set aside as a shield before you invest heavy.

5. **Scams & Fake "Opportunities"**

- Shady courses, "double your money fast" promises, sketchy crypto coins.

- **Truth:** If it sounds too good to be true, it probably is.

🔒 Protecting the Bag: Smart Habits

1. **Separate Accounts**

- Keep hustle money, bills, and investments in different places.

- Makes it harder to "accidentally" spend what's meant to grow.

2. **Track & Audit**

- Review your money weekly.

- If you don't know where your dollars are, someone else is controlling them.

3. **Insure & Secure**

- Insurance for car, health, or business gear.

- Password protection, 2FA, and cybersecurity if you hustle online.

4. Think Long-Term

- Don't blow today's bag for a quick flex.
- Every dollar has a job — to protect, multiply, or create opportunities.

💡 Everyday Millionaire Mindset

Poor Kid chases money but loses it just as fast.

Rich Kid builds systems to **keep and grow** money.

Protecting the bag doesn't feel exciting in the moment — but trust me, nothing feels better than knowing your money is safe, working for you, and untouchable by the usual traps.

🏁 Part 4:

Beyond $1,000

🏗 Chapter 11:
From Hustler to Builder – Turning $1,000 Into $10,000

Making $1,000 is your first big win. Keeping it was your second. But now comes the real test: **turning that $1,000 into $10,000.**

This is where hustlers graduate into builders. Hustlers chase quick wins. Builders create systems, investments, and habits that multiply money consistently.

🔑 Step 1: Shift from Hustle Mode to Builder Mode

- **Hustler Thinking:** "How do I make $100 fast?"
- **Builder Thinking:** "How do I create a system that pays me $100 over and over?"
- The builder mindset takes you from short-term sprints to long-term marathons.

💼 Step 2: Reinvest in Scalable Hustles

Your $1,000 can fuel bigger plays:

- **E-commerce Store** → buy inventory, run ads, reinvest profits.
- **Freelancing** → upgrade tools, market better, land higher-paying clients.
- **Local Business** → equipment for cleaning, landscaping, catering, or delivery.
- **Digital Products** → create ebooks, courses, or templates that can sell infinitely.

💡 **Rule:** If it doesn't scale, it stalls.

📊 Step 3: Use the Power of Multiplication

Instead of blowing $1,000 on one risky move, split it into a **3-part formula:**

1. **50% Growth Hustle** − reinvest in what's already working.
2. **30% Long-Term Investment** − index funds, ETFs, or skill-building.
3. **20% Safety Net** − cash reserve for emergencies.

This way, you grow without gambling everything.

🚀 Step 4: Build Consistency & Systems

- Schedule your hustle time like a job.

- Track income and expenses.

- Use tools and automation (social media schedulers, payment systems, apps).

- Build repeat customers instead of chasing new ones every time.

Consistency is what takes $1,000 one time and turns it into $10,000 every year.

⚫ Step 5: Expand Your Vision

Think bigger. Instead of asking, *"How do I make more money?"* ask:

- "Who can I partner with to grow faster?"

- "What systems can I automate?"

- "How can I add value to more people at once?"

This is how you move from grinding to **building wealth.**

Example: The $1,000 to $10,000 Play

1. Hustler earns $1,000 dog-walking.

2. Builder reinvests $500 in marketing + $300 in insurance + $200 in gear.

3. Lands 20 repeat clients → earns $10,000+ that year.

It's not magic. It's mindset + reinvestment + consistency.

💡 Everyday Millionaire Mindset

Poor Kid spends $1,000 and has nothing to show for it.

Hustler makes $1,000 and celebrates too long.

Rich Kid turns $1,000 into $10,000, and then into **freedom.**

Your $1,000 is the seed. What you plant today determines if it grows into a tree, or if it rots in the soil.

✳️ Chapter 12:
Everyday Millionaire Habits — Staying on the Path

By now, you've hustled, stacked, protected, and multiplied your first $1,000. That's a milestone worth celebrating — but it's not the finish line. The real win is building the **habits that keep you on the path to financial freedom, every single day.**

🌀 1. Keep the Mindset Strong

- Rich Kid thinking says: "Money is a tool, not a trophy."
- Always see opportunities, even in small places.
- Stay focused on building, not flexing.

💹 2. Pay Yourself First

- Every dollar that comes in → invest, save, or stack before you spend.
- Make it automatic. The habit matters more than the amount.

🕐 3. Master Time Like the Rich

- Poor Kid wastes time scrolling.
- Rich Kid sees time as currency — invests it into skills, hustles, and relationships.
- Daily planner > daily excuses.

🛡️ 4. Protect Your Bag at All Costs

- Guard against lifestyle creep, scams, and unnecessary debt.
- Keep your emergency fund strong.
- Stay disciplined — defense is just as important as offense.

📚 5. Learn Forever

- Millionaires never stop being students.
- Read books, listen to podcasts, study money, and surround yourself with people who challenge you to grow.

🌐 6. Build Relationships That Build Wealth

- Network smart: mentors, collaborators, partners.

- Who you hang around determines what you normalize — poverty or prosperity.

🩶 7. Health, Balance & Giving Back

- Health is wealth — energy fuels the hustle.
- Don't burn out; balance hustle with rest and renewal.
- Generosity keeps your money mindset healthy — give, and opportunities return multiplied.

💡 Everyday Millionaire Mindset

Your first $1,000 was proof.

Your next $10,000 is potential.

But your habits? They're **forever.**

If you keep stacking the right habits daily — saving, investing, learning, networking, and protecting your bag — you'll look up one day and realize you're not just hustling anymore. You're living the millionaire lifestyle you once only dreamed of.

Bonus Sections

📖 Glossary of Hustle & Money Terms

- **Asset** – Anything that puts money in your pocket (business, investment, rental).

- **Liability** – Anything that takes money out of your pocket (debt, unnecessary expenses).

- **Cash Flow** – The movement of money in and out of your life or business.

- **Compound Interest** – The "snowball effect" of money earning money over time.

- **Diversify** – Spreading money across multiple income streams or investments to reduce risk.

- **Emergency Fund** – Cash savings to cover unexpected costs without using credit.

- **Index Fund / ETF** – A basket of stocks you buy into for safe, long-term growth.

- **Passive Income** – Money you earn while not actively working (rent, royalties, dividends).

- **ROI (Return on Investment)** – How much you make back compared to what you put in.

- **Side Hustle** – A money-making project outside your main job.

- **Stacking** – Building money step by step, keeping the habit strong.

- **Wealth Mindset** – Thinking long-term, using money as a tool, not just for spending.

💡 100 Ideas to Make Your First $1,000

(Fast-hit list to spark action — no fluff, just options.)

Online Hustles

1. Freelance writing
2. Graphic design
3. Social media management
4. Virtual assistant work
5. Video editing
6. Selling on eBay
7. Print-on-demand t-shirts
8. Dropshipping store
9. YouTube channel monetization
10. Affiliate marketing

Creative Hustles

11. Photography sessions
12. Tutoring music
13. Etsy crafts

14. Voiceover gigs

15. Art commissions

16. Podcast editing

17. Copywriting

18. Resume services

19. Translation work

20. Blogging (ads & sponsors)

Service Hustles

21. Babysitting

22. Dog walking

23. House cleaning

24. Lawn care

25. Snow shoveling

26. Junk removal

27. Delivery driver

28. Handyman services

29. Moving help

30. Car detailing

Product Hustles

31. Baking/catering

32. Farmers market booth

33. Thrift flipping

34. Candle making

35. Soap/skincare line

36. Jewelry making

37. Furniture flipping

38. Meal prep service

39. Merch reselling

40. Pop-up shops

Passive & Semi-Passive Hustles

41. Sell an ebook

42. Create a course

43. License your photography

44. Publish a low-content book

45. Build a subscription box

46. Invest in stocks/ETFs

47. Rent out a spare room

48. Peer-to-peer lending

49. Create paid templates

50. Start a Patreon

Local/Community Hustles

51. Car wash service

52. Event planning

53. DJing

54. Bartending for events

55. Face painting

56. Balloon twisting

57. Fitness coaching

58. Personal training

59. Tutoring students

60. Language lessons

Tech Hustles

61. App testing

62. Bug bounty hunting

63. Tech setup for seniors

64. WordPress site builds

65. SEO optimization

66. Online ads management

67. Shopify store building

68. Chatbot creation

69. Freelance coding

70. UX/UI design

Seasonal Hustles

71. Holiday decorating

72. Pumpkin patch stand

73. Valentine's gift baskets

74. Summer yard care

75. Back-to-school tutoring

76. Tax prep help

77. Spring cleaning services

78. Graduation photography

79. Costume rentals

80. Snow plowing

Event & Entertainment Hustles

81. Karaoke hosting

82. Open mic nights

83. Dance lessons

84. Party photography

85. Wedding planning assistant

86. Craft fair booth

87. Photo booth rentals

88. Catering desserts

89. Bounce house rental

90. Children's party entertainment

Everyday Hustles

91. Selling unused clothes

92. Renting out tools

93. Selling gift cards

94. Delivery for local restaurants

95. Carpool driving

96. Recycling for cash

97. Freelance research

98. Mystery shopping

99. Paid surveys (extra cash filler)

100. Teaching workshops

♀ **Pro Tip:** Don't just pick one. Try a mix, double down on what pays, and stack fast.

About the Author

Anthony Carmichael is a creator, entrepreneur, and motivator dedicated to helping people turn ideas into income and hustles into wealth. Through his **Rich Kid, Poor Kid** series, Anthony breaks down money, mindset, and business in a way that's real, practical, and motivating.

He knows what it's like to start with little and build from the ground up — and his mission is simple: **teach the everyday hustler how to win.** Whether through books, workshops, or digital platforms, Anthony inspires readers to take action, build discipline, and chase freedom with courage and faith.

🔥 Final Message:
The First $1,000 Is Just the Beginning

You did it. You learned the plays, the habits, and the mindset. You know how to hustle, stack, protect, and grow. Your first $1,000 isn't just money in the bank — it's **proof** you can change your life.

But remember this: $1,000 is just the spark. What you do next turns it into $10,000... into $100,000... into the life you dream about.

Stay focused. Stay disciplined. Keep hustling smart. Because the everyday millionaire path isn't about luck — it's about building brick by brick until freedom is yours.

💡 Now go get it — your future self is already thanking you.

✂ Download Extra Worksheets

Want templates, trackers, planners, and business tools?

We've got you covered. Visit:

👉

www.richkidpoorkidbooks.com/worksheetsandtemplates

There, you can download:

- Business plan templates

- Budget + finance trackers

- Social media calendars

- Contract + invoice samples

- Branding guides

    ... and more!

Visit Our Website

⊞ Scan the QR code below or visit

www.RichKidPoorKidBooks.com to access:

- Free worksheets & templates

- Bonus lessons and digital downloads

- Exclusive community updates

- Upcoming book releases and programs

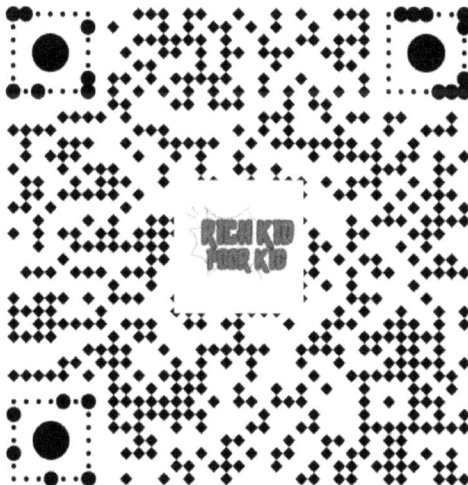

Join the movement. Learn. Build. Become.

Rich Kid Academy — where knowledge becomes power.

www.ingramcontent.com/pod-product-compliance
Lightning Source LLC
Chambersburg PA
CBHW060644210326
41520CB00010B/1730